Huong's Journey

by Frank Hartley

NATIONAL GEOGRAPHIC LEARNING | CENGAGE

This is Huong. She is an artist.

Huong paints pictures.

In 1975, Huong lived in Saigon.
Saigon is a city in Vietnam.

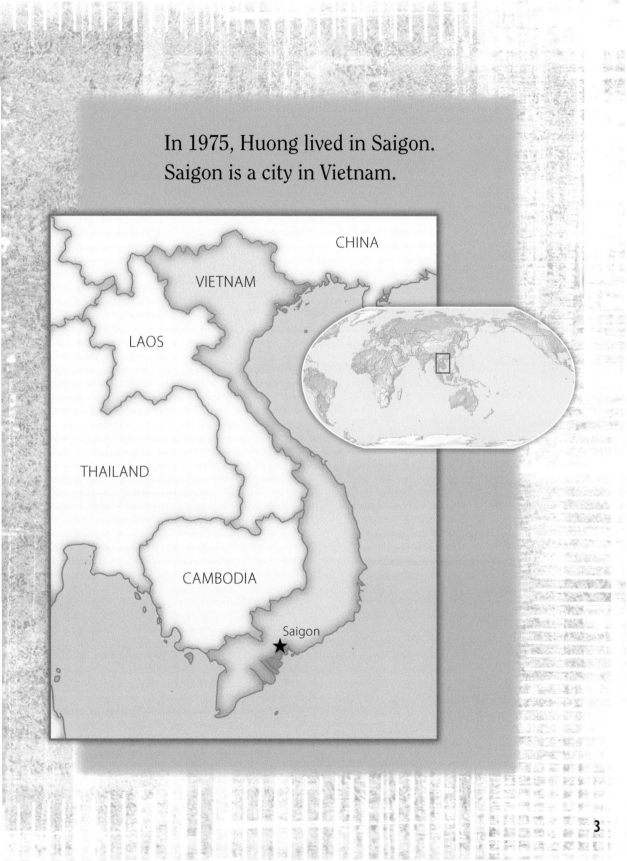

It was dangerous to live in Vietnam in 1975. There was a terrible war there.

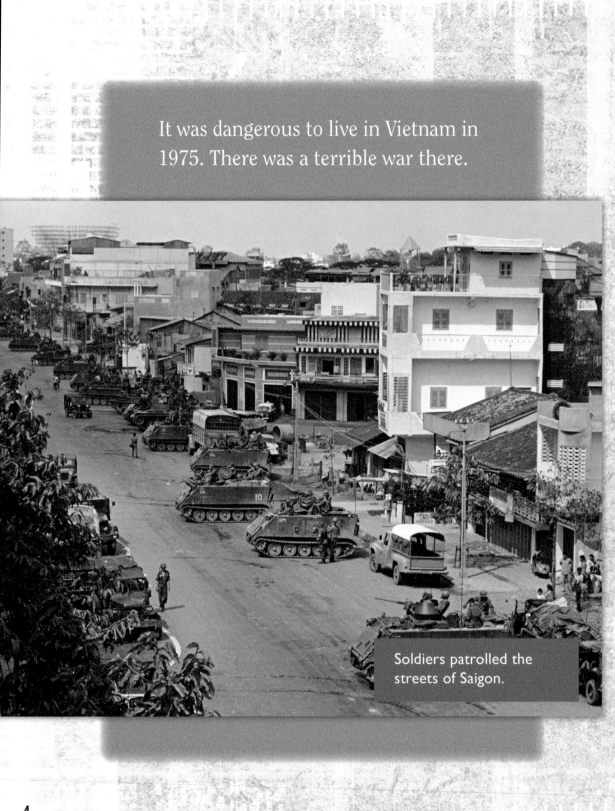

Soldiers patrolled the streets of Saigon.

Huong wanted to take her son away from the war. She and her son left.

Thousands of people left Saigon.

Huong and her son left Vietnam
on a small boat.

The boat trip was very
dangerous.

They came to the United States to start a new life.

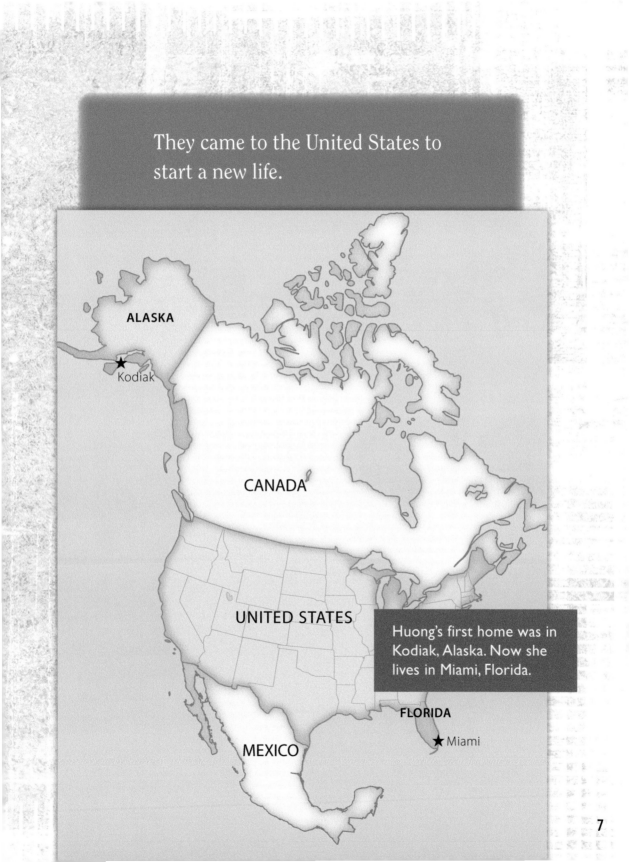

ALASKA

★ Kodiak

CANADA

UNITED STATES

Huong's first home was in Kodiak, Alaska. Now she lives in Miami, Florida.

FLORIDA

★ Miami

MEXICO

In Vietnam, Huong was a writer.

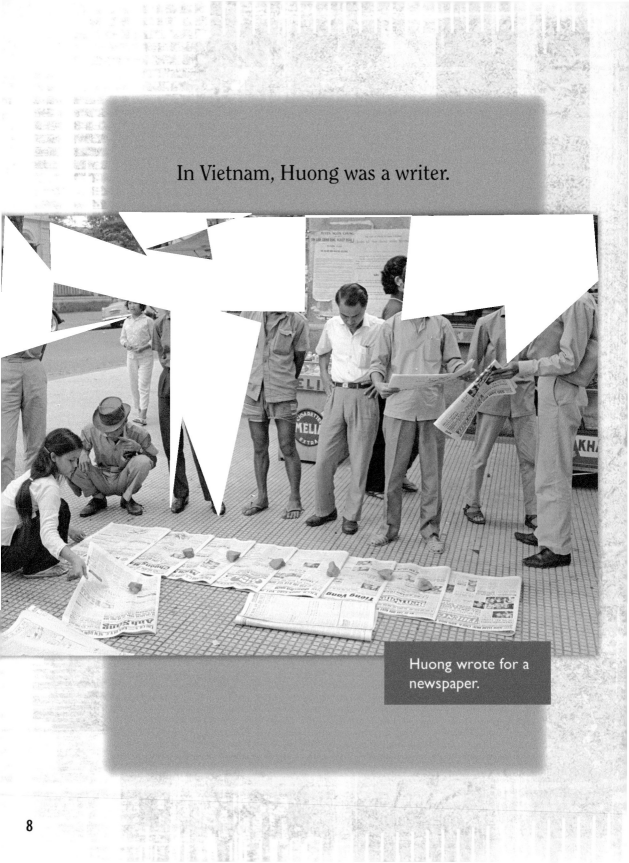

Huong wrote for a newspaper.

In the United States, Huong is a painter.

Huong shares her ideas by writing and by painting.

Huong's memories of Vietnam help her paint. Her life in the United States helps her paint, too.

Huong paints her memories. She paints her experiences.

Huong's paintings are about war.

Huong uses many shapes
and colors in her paintings.

They are also about peace.

Many people come to see
Huong's paintings.

Now Huong is working on a peace mural.

The mural has 2,000 paintings.
It is 8 feet tall and 600 feet long.

Huong's art reminds us that peace is important.